THE
GUADALUPE
HISTORIC FOUNDATION

To Ginger & Leo

My OLD Friends

Edward L. Gonzales

Gonzo 3/15/2017

THE
GUADALUPE
HISTORIC FOUNDATION

*How a Secular, Non-profit Organization
Saved Santa Fe's Most Religious Site*

Kay Lockridge

SUNSTONE
PRESS

SANTA FE

Note: All information current as of the date of the publication of this book.

.

Sunstone books may be purchased for educational, business, or sales promotional use.
For information please write: Special Markets Department, Sunstone Press,
P.O. Box 2321, Santa Fe, New Mexico 87504-2321.

Body typeface › Minion Pro
Printed on acid-free paper
∞
eBook 978-1-61139-492-4

Library of Congress Cataloging-in-Publication Data

On File

SUNSTONE PRESS IS COMMITTED TO MINIMIZING OUR ENVIRONMENTAL IMPACT ON THE PLANET. THE PAPER USED IN THIS BOOK IS FROM
RESPONSIBLY MANAGED FORESTS. OUR PRINTER HAS RECEIVED CHAIN OF CUSTODY (COC) CERTIFICATION FROM: THE FOREST STEWARDSHIP
COUNCIL™ (FSC®), PROGRAMME FOR THE ENDORSEMENT OF FOREST CERTIFICATION™ (PEFC™), AND THE SUSTAINABLE FORESTRY INITIATIVE® (SFI®).
THE FSC® COUNCIL IS A NON-PROFIT ORGANIZATION, PROMOTING THE ENVIRONMENTALLY APPROPRIATE, SOCIALLY BENEFICIAL AND
ECONOMICALLY VIABLE MANAGEMENT OF THE WORLD'S FORESTS. FSC® CERTIFICATION IS RECOGNIZED INTERNATIONALLY AS A
RIGOROUS ENVIRONMENTAL AND SOCIAL STANDARD FOR RESPONSIBLE FOREST MANAGEMENT.

WWW.SUNSTONEPRESS.COM
SUNSTONE PRESS / POST OFFICE BOX 2321 / SANTA FE, NM 87504-2321 /USA
(505) 988-4418 / ORDERS ONLY (800) 243-5644 / FAX (505) 988-1025

DEDICATION

This book is dedicated to Spanish Colonial historian Gabrielle Palmer, who had the foresight, wisdom and energy to lead the effort to save the Santuario de Guadalupe when others wanted to tear it down and put up a parking lot. The Guadalupe Historic Foundation was the result, and we are forever grateful to all who followed her: staff, members, volunteers and donors who kept the dream alive over the years and saved the Santuario de Guadalupe.

CONTENTS

Leo Kahn, who presided over the last five years of the Guadalupe Historic Foundation, which concluded its work on January 31, 2006, took this photograph of Our
Lady of Guadalupe superimposed on a recent photograph of the Santuario.

Preface

The Santuario de Guadalupe, The Miracle Becomes Real

*M*iracles don't come easy. In fact, most don't come at all. So, when a miracle does occur, it's important to take note. This is the story of the Guadalupe Historic Foundation, from beginning to end.

It's also a tale about two men, separated by time and place yet on the same quest in search of a miracle: Juan Diego and Edward Gonzales—almost 500 years apart—one who witnessed the miracle of Our Lady of Guadalupe in Her appearance in Spanish-colonized Mexico in the first half of the 16th century to the other who played a key role in the salvation of the Santuario de Guadalupe, created in Her honor in Northern New Mexico in the last quarter of the 20th century.

Two men could not be more different, except for their Roman Catholic faith. Juan Diego was a poor, uneducated peasant in the countryside of Mexico City when he witnessed four visions of Our Lady of Guadalupe on a hill outside Mexico City in December, 1531. Diego had converted to Roman Catholicism when the Spanish arrived 10 years earlier. It had offered him and other indigenous inhabitants relief from the harsh practices and beliefs of the Aztecs.

The apparition, which he first saw on December 9th, instructed Diego to go to the Basilica Guadalupe in nearby Mexico City and ask the Bishop to build a chapel on Tepeyac Hill, where the visions occurred. Twice, the Bishop rebuffed Diego, finally telling him to produce evidence of Our Lady's appearance and request.

Diego relayed the Bishop's request to Our Lady, whereupon She told him to return to her the fourth day—December 12—and receive the desired sign. He did so and found the hillside covered with beautiful roses in the dead of winter. Having nothing to carry them in for the short journey to the Bishop, Diego removed his tilma, or cloak, and swept up the roses.

Upon reaching the Basilica Guadalupe, Diego opened the tilma, thereby spilling the roses over the floor at the Bishop's feet. At the same time, the image of the Holy Mother appeared on the cloak and remains there to this day.

The chapel was built on Tepeyac Hill, and December 12 was proclaimed Our Lady of Guadalupe Feast Day. This part of the story comes full circle in 2002 when Juan Diego was declared a saint, and December 9 is known as the Feast of Juan Diego in the Roman Catholic Church. At the same time, December 12th is celebrated annually as the Feast Day of Our Lady of Guadalupe throughout Mexico and the American Southwest.

Moving forward to the third quarter of the 20th century, the story continues in Santa Fe, New Mexico, where Edward Gonzales would never call himself a saint; yet, there are parallels with Juan Diego and his quest.

Working within in and for the community comes naturally to this Norteno, whose roots run deep in Northern New Mexico. Gonzales is the youngest and only surviving sibling of the 12 children born to Leopoldo and Elizabeth Fayette Gonzales. His mother, who served as New Mexico Secretary of State, came from a family of French trappers who arrived in New Mexico in the 19th century. Edward's family helped settle Santa Fe in the 17th century.

Both parents and most of his siblings were active in the community throughout their lives. Edward Gonzales had little choice but to follow suit. He briefly served on the Santa Fe City Council and was an active member of the Santa Fe Fiesta Council for 25 years.

It's his work on behalf of the 225-year-old Santuario de Guadalupe Chapel—the oldest still-active shrine to Our Lady in the United States—that both invigorates and haunts him. He asserts that the existence of the Santuario is a result of a series of small miracles that occurred, as miracles usually do, at just the right time.

The first modern-day miracle was the creation of the Santuario Historic Foundation, a secular, non-profit organization, in 1975. By that time, the Santuario was falling into disrepair, and many members of the Guadalupe parish wanted to demolish the old building and add on to the main church's parking lot.

Citizens of all persuasions came together in the foundation to protect and preserve the Santuario. One of those citizens was Edward Gonzales, who had been married to Pat Gonzales y Gonzales in the Santuario in 1959. (Guadalupe was her family's parish, while Edward and his family attended St. Francis Cathedral—now the Cathedral Basilica of St. Francis of Assisi, which Pat and Edward attend today.)

"This structure (the Santuario) anchored the early Santa Fe community," Gonzales asserts. "It has meaning for all those who have ever lived in and loved Santa Fe. Other buildings in the City Different may be more beautiful, but none contains the history of Old and New Mexico together. The Santuario is the heart of Santa Fe."

Over the next 25 years, Gonzales observed and recorded these miracles, including contributions of time, effort and money that seemed to come "just in the nick of time," he says.

"It really is a miracle that the Santuario has survived when you consider all the different personalities, beliefs and agendas of the thousands of people who have been involved in the Foundation and its efforts over the years," Gonzales notes. "Miracles happen when you least expect them but always when you need them. The Santuario de Guadalupe is proof of that."

One of the earliest photos of the Santuario de Guadalupe, taken in the 19th Century, shows a mule-drawn cart in front of the edifice. William Henry Jackson. Courtesy of the Palace of the Governors Photo Archives (NMHM/DCA), 132561.

City Councilman Edward Gonzales, right, presents a proclamation commending the planned preservation of the Santuario de Guadalupe to Guadalupe Historic Foundation co-founders, Rev. Leo Lucero, left, and Gabrielle Palmer, who also served as the project director, and Saul Cohen, Foundation trustee. Gonzales made the presentation on behalf of Santa Fe Mayor Joseph E. Valdes. Photograph by Jeff Moscow, *The Santa Fe New Mexican,* June 30, 1975.

Taken in 1910, this photograph shows the effects of the remodeling carried out under Father De Fouri in 1881, reflecting the New England influence. The bell tower had been torn down, the adobe walls raised and a steeple placed on top of a dramatically slanted roof. The low, square door was replaced by a narrower, vertical combination door and window. Courtesy of the Palace of the Governors Photo Archives (NMHM/DCA), 051308.

The Santuario de Guadalupe in the 1920s with the narrow-gauge railroad tracks in front. T. Harmon Parkhurst. Santuario de Guadalupe, Santa Fe, New Mexico. Courtesy of the Palace of the Governors Photo Archives (NMHM/DCA), 010036.

The Santuario as it appeared in the 1930s. Guadalupe Church, Santa Fe, New Mexico. T. Harmon Parkhurst. Guadalupe Church, Santa Fe, New Mexico. Courtesy of the Palace of the Governors Photo Archives (NMHM/DCA), 010038.

A stone wall replaced a picket fence, with the archway complementing the arches of the new bell tower that had replaced the steeple, which had been destroyed in the 1922 fire. The railroad tracks, which had been laid in the late 19th Century, were removed in the early 1940s. Courtesy of the Palace of the Governors Photo Archives (NMHM/DCA), 015043.

Our Lady of Guadalupe is the patron saint of Mexico, and the influence of that nation's culture is evident in the architecture and decoration of the Santuario de Guadalupe. Circa 1942 from the book, Santa Fe, by Ernest Knee.

High on the trestle, the narrow-gauge Chile Line train steams past the Santuario de Guadalupe northbound in 1941. The line subsequently was discontinued and the tracks dismantled. Margaret McKittrick. The Denver and Rio Grande, 1941, Courtesy of the Palace of the Governors Photo Archives (NMHM/DCA), 041833.

With each renovation of the interior of the Santuario de Guadalupe, the altar became
more ornate and the Santuario itself more user friendly. The original chapel, for
instance, had dirt floors and no pews. There also was no altar railing to separate
the sanctuary. (Note the antiquated, convoluted heating system.) On continuous
display, however, is the 1783 painting by Jose de Alzibar picturing Our Lady
surrounded by four scenes depicting the miracle of her appearance to Juan Diego
in Spanish-colonized Mexico in the 16th Century. T. Harmon Parkhurst. Church
Interior, Santuario de Guadalupe, Santa Fe, New Mexico. Courtesy of the
Palace of the Governors Photo Archives (NMHM/DCA), 010035.

Foreword

The Foundation Begins as the Santuario is About to End

*A*s the seventh decade of the 20th century draws to a close, the Archdiocese of Santa Fe declares that the almost-200-year-old Santuario de Guadalupe should be demolished before it falls down of its own volition. In fact, the parish wants to expand the parking lot into the space occupied by the adobe artifact.

Not so fast, commands then-Archbishop Robert Sanchez. Many of Santa Fe's Roman Catholics, some of whom had been parishioners of and even married in the old Our Lady of Guadalupe Church and were no longer part of the parish, want to see the original Santuario preserved for future generations.

Since there are no funds for such a massive effort, the Archbishop turns to the community at large for help. Thus is born the Guadalupe Historic Foundation in 1975. Its mission is simple yet daunting: bring the 18th century Santuario into the 20th century and prepare it for the 21st century and beyond. To accomplish this, the Archdiocese turned the deed to the property containing the Santuario and immediate surrounding area over to the Foundation.

It no longer will be a church but a historic building that will house and present the music, art and culture of the City of Faith. Stepping up to the plate are the new Guadalupe Parish priest, Father Leo Lucero, and a concerned citizen, historian Gabrielle Palmer. Together, they create the secular Guadalupe Historic Foundation and, with a study grant from the New Mexico Arts Commission, they begin what will become the process of restoration.

Because the Foundation is a secular, not-for-profit organization, there is no problem of public funds going to a religious group so grants may be sought from all levels of government—city, state and federal—as well as other public and private sources. For the latter group, contributions from individuals are tax deductible.

Gabrielle Palmer has long been interested in the Santuario and its place in the story of Santa Fe. With a PhD in Spanish Colonial art in hand from the University of New Mexico, she believes that the City Different needs to step up to its place in history.

In fact, upon her return from travels in Spain and South America, she tells *The Santa Fe New Mexican* (in 1976), "the one indigenous form besides Indian art in this area of the country (is) Spanish Colonial, and yet it was curiously not readily available to the community (of Santa Fe).

"Museums can be such self-effacing structures in which to house art, whereas Spanish Colonial art actually existed in a whole cultural framework, mostly within the church. I want to find a way for the art to live on its own, where exhibits could be interpretive and coherent...in a place like the Santuario.

"There is a very spiritual sense to the art of the Spanish Colonial period. Everything surrounding the works, including the church, the people and the faith were a part of them, giving meaning to every element within the art.

"The idea is to bring the elements back together again. It's more than an integration," Palmer stresses. "It's also surrounding the art with people and feeling, so that the art comes to life again."

Palmer adds today that when she drove by the Santuario back then, "I felt badly at its deterioration and thought, 'if that's what it looks like on the outside, I shudder to think what must be happening inside.'"

The Foundation, with its all-volunteer board and membership drawn from the community, goes to work. While the parish and the Archdiocese are pleased to see the work commence, they play no part in the effort in terms of financial aid or direction.

Once she and Father Leo got the OK from Archbishop Sanchez, Palmer says she took two steps: applied for and received a $170,000 grant from the federal Housing and Urban Development (thanks to then-New Mexico Sen. Manuel Lujan) and engaged local architect Nathaniel Owings as a consultant for the restoration project.

Other grants of varying size came from the New Mexico Arts Commission, the New Mexico American Revolutionary Bicentennial Commission, the City of Santa Fe's Community development Commission, as well as local service clubs.

"We went into high gear and put the Foundation into operation once the money started coming in," Palmer adds. It turned out that the interior of the Santuario, about which she had worried so much, "was the great thing... absolutely beautiful, pristine. I was so grateful to be in a project of such worth and beauty. It was an honor to be a part of it."

(It should be noted that the name Guadalupe itself has a fascinating history. It initially designated a river in the Spanish province of Extremadura and is thought to derive from Arabic—spoken by the Moors, who ruled the Spanish Peninsula for 800 years—and Latin—spoken by the Romans who ruled before them. It was called the River of Wolves. The name became famous in the 14th century as a result of an apparition of the Blessed Virgin Mary in the Spanish town of Guadalupe, with the resulting pilgrimages and a statue commemorating the vision.

(Both the apparition and statue became known as Our Lady of Guadalupe and now are called Our Lady of Guadalupe, Extremadura or, sometimes, Our Lady of Extremadura.

(Others have suggested the name originated in Mexico in the 16th century and is a corruption of a word in the indigenous language, Nahuatl, which was the native tongue of Juan Diego, who experienced visions of the Blessed Mother on a hill outside Mexico City.

(Spanish Conquistador Hernando Cortez had conquered Mexico City and dislodged the Aztecs, installing both the Roman Catholic faith and Spanish governance over the local population. Cortez was from the Spanish enclave of Extremadura, and he subsequently created the Basilica Guadalupe in Mexico City.)

When they arrived in what became New Mexico, the Spanish created the first of four villas or towns—La Villa Real de la Santa Fe de San Francisco de Assisi/The Royal Town of the Holy Faith of St. Francis of Assisi—and Santa Fe became the focal point of the Spanish in New Mexico in the 17th century.

Laid out according to Spanish plan, the town surrounded a central plaza with streets radiating from the plaza. In turn, the Guadalupe Barrio—an administrative unit created by the Spanish with ill-defined boundaries—focused on the Chapel of our Lady of Guadalupe built at what then was the end of the Camino Real, the royal road from Mexico City. It remains so today, as the parish and barrio practically are interchangeable.

Created almost as a suburb of Santa Fe, the Barrio grew in the early 19th century around and to the west of the Chapel. According to local historian Marc Simmons, there were a few houses and numerous cornfields in the middle colonial period. It was, and remains, primarily a working class neighborhood.

Farmers and day laborers comprised the largest categories of inhabitants, with a few masons, silversmiths, cobblers, shepherds, carpenters and tailors scattered throughout the area. A census of 1823 even lists a beggar among the residents. By 1841, however, the barrio population included several families prominent in the business and political life of the province.

Simmons says the route of the Camino Real most likely originated as an Indian trail extending from the pueblos along the Rio Grande from Mexico to the vicinity of the present community of Agua Fria and the Sangre de Cristo Mountains east of Santa Fe. The road ultimately led to the central plaza to the northeast of the Santuario.

The Camino Real crossed the Rio Chiquito, or Santa Fe River, in front of the Chapel, followed in the late 19th century by the so-called Chili Line, a narrow-gauge railroad run by the Denver and Rio Grande Western Railroad. The Chili Line ran from Espanola south into Santa Fe from 1887 to 1941, when it was disbanded. Photos from the 1940s show the trestle running in front of the Chapel.

After Mexico gained its independence from Spain in 1821, the road's name of Camino Real was changed to Camino Nacional in keeping with the new republican form of government. The people of the Guadalupe Barrio apparently continued to use the familiar name of Camino Real, and Simmons says it appeared in deeds and other legal documents to the end of the 19th century. Ultimately, the Guadalupe Barrio became Agua Fria. At about the same time, the road running immediately in front of the Santuario Chapel became Guadalupe Street in honor of the parish and the Santuario.

By the mid-20th century, the barrio was one of the few parts of Santa Fe, outside the Canyon Road district, in which many fine, old-style adobes were still standing. One of the latter in the Guadalupe area was the Manuel Antonio Chaves home that, almost 50 years ago, served as the rectory for the newly built Our Lady of Guadalupe Church that succeeded the Santuario de Guadalupe in 1961.

Today, day laborers—most from Mexico—can be seen in front of the Santuario every day looking for work. The parish continues to serve these folks and those who live in the immediate area. The Santuario, which used to present art exhibits, musical shows and other community-oriented activities, still draws locals and visitors to Santa Fe.

"If it weren't for the Foundation, we wouldn't be here today," says the current director of the Santuario, Gail Delgado. "The most important thing is that it brings the community together." Delgado also staffs the Santuario shop, offering devotional and historical items for sale to help support the upkeep.

The early church, estimated to have been built sometime between 1776 and 1795, was typical of 18th century New Mexico indigenous architecture. Built in the shape of a Latin cross, the nave measured approximately 70 feet in length, the arms of the transept about 30 feet. The building itself was constructed of large adobe bricks forming a wall about 33 inches thick.

Small, high windows were recessed in the walls and covered with wooden grills. The floor was packed dirt. Vigas, solid pine logs, formed the ceiling and rested on double corbels decorated with a simple, incised pattern.

The choir loft spanned the nave at the face and was supported by a huge, square beam bearing the scratched inscription: "un padre nuestro un ave maria por amor a dios" (exact translation into English undetermined) and signed by "Antonio de Jesusero," who may have been the foreman in charge of the construction work. The interior walls were plastered with adobe mud and finished with a coat of white gesso, local gypsum and macaceous clay.

The exterior also was plastered with adobe. The flat roof was drained by a series of large wooden gutters, and its massive fortress-like exterior was set off by a small square three-tiered bell tower that adjoined the building to the southeast. A burial ground surrounded the church, encircled by a low adobe wall.

Designated a chapel by the Archdiocese, the Santuario de Guadalupe was situated at some distance from St. Francis Cathedral, the parish church, and served the needs of those who lived nearby. There were no regular services originally, although parish priests may have celebrated monthly masses, as well as the Feast Day of Our Lady of Guadalupe December 12th.

By 1817, the chapel was in serious disrepair. In 1826, the Archdiocese determined that the adobe building could not be used as a House of God.

The Santuario virtually was vacant until 1881, when Archbishop Jean Baptiste Lamy declared that the Santuario would be under the care of Father James H. DeFouri and used for the English-speaking (American) Catholic population that had been pouring into Santa Fe since 1846.

Repairs commenced, and the Santuario became the church of English-speaking parishioners led by Father DeFouri. Following a Victorian style reflecting the influx of Anglo parishioners from the East, the flat roof was replaced with a pitched roof, atop which perched a cupola containing a 575-pound bell and an orange-colored spire. A second bell was added at the end of the 19th century. Neo-Gothic windows were placed in the walls around that time.

Santuario de Guadalupe continued to serve as a parish church until 1918 when, once again, it became an auxiliary to the Cathedral parish that served both Spanish- and English-speaking parishioners. A fire in 1922 razed the roof, with the spire near collapse and painted frescoes inside destroyed. The adobe walls and altar survived.

Restoration in a California mission style followed, and heavy, random-width pine planking replaced the packed dirt. The Santuario returned to full-fledged parish status in 1931 as Santa Fe's population grew.

By the late 1950s, the Guadalupe parish had outgrown the Santuario, and a new, much larger church was built on the extended site and dedicated in 1961. The Santuario was used for various secular activities from 1961 to 1975 but fell into deterioration, which is what Archbishop Sanchez lamented and Gabrielle Palmer saw as she drove by the Santuario daily in the early 1970s.

Ultimately, it was decided to return the Santuario to its 18th century origin with modern construction methods, materials and tools. Those efforts, their results and the individuals who created them will be related in future chapters.

Greeting visitors to the Santuario was, and is, a large altar screen painted by renowned Mexican Colonial artist Jose de Alzibar in 1783. It depicts the Virgin of Guadalupe surrounded by four colorful vignettes that relate the various moments of the miraculous apparition of our lady to Juan Diego. (It is said that Our Lady saved the Santuario from destruction because it was part of the western wall of the structure and could not be removed without great expense.)

Before the massive renovation began in 1976, the Santuario was in a sorry state. The stained glass windows that had been installed above the entrance after the fire in 1922 were either broken or removed to preserve them and replaced by wood panels. A workman is shown entering the front door during the renovation. Photograph by Steve McDowell, *The Santa Fe New Mexican*, December 5, 1976.

When surface features such as the pillars were stripped away—revealing vigas that supported the choir loft, a long horizontal beam across the top of the doorway and an older and broader door jam—a replica was made of the window on top of the door and the hole that formerly held a clock was filled in with adobe bricks. The boundary of the door was widened to conform to the measurements of the frame. Photograph by Steve McDowell, *The Santa Fe New Mexican,* December 5, 1976.

Completed doorway built by Thayer Carter. The hand-forged iron hardware was made by Frank Turley who modeled the hardware from the design of other iron products from the Colonial period. The proportion was restored to the building, and the rough surface gave a more earthy appearance to the exterior—later to be covered with a final coat of plaster. Photograph by Dennis Dahl, *The Santa Fe New Mexican,* December 5, 1976.

Exterior restoration of Santuario de Guadalupe, Santa Fe, New Mexico, 1991. Courtesy of the Palace of the Governors Photo Archives (NMHM/DCA), HP.2014.14.1407. (From *The Santa Fe New Mexican* Collection.)

Detail of the Santuario during renovation/reconstruction in 1976. Arthur Taylor. Santuario de Guadalupe, Santa Fe, New Mexico. Courtesy of the Palace of the Governors Photo Archives (NMHM/DCA), 112108.

In 1976, the high Gothic windows were filled in with adobe brick and the square ones built by the Spanish colonists exposed. Extra height was achieved by vigas supported by corbals. Arthur Taylor. Architectural Detail, Santuario de Guadalupe, Santa Fe, New Mexico. Courtesy of the Palace of the Governors Photo Archives (NMHM/DCA), 112113.

Construction continues on the exterior of the Santuario in 1976. Note the exposed adobe above the doorway and the inset of Our Lady to the right of the door. Arthur Taylor. Exposed adobe, Santuario de Guadalupe, Guadalupe Street, Santa Fe, New Mexico. Courtesy of the Palace of the Governors Photo Archives (NMHM/DCA), 117124

Winter enhanced this scene of the Santuario in 1976, and spring would see the newly planted trees blossoming next to the new fountain. The approach and footpaths were constructed and trimmed to create a reflective mood for visitors. Photograph by Dennis Dahl, *The Santa Fe New Mexican,* December 5, 1976.

The Santuario as it appeared in the early 1970s. David Donoho. Santuario de Guadalupe in Snow, Santa Fe, New Mexico. Courtesy of the Palace of the Governors Photo Archives (NMHM/DCA), 156842.

The interior of the Santuario from the choir loft. Sunlight was captured by carefully placed windows. Photograph by Dennis Dahl, *The Santa Fe New Mexican,* December 5, 1976.

1

The Money Begins Flowing

*T*he following are recollections of Edward "Gonzo" Gonzales. He was there in 1974-75 as a City Councilman and concerned citizen when the Guadalupe Historic Foundation began and subsequently became an active member of the Foundation in 1978. Edward Gonzales then took a break in 1982 and resumed membership on the Foundation board from 1985 to 2001.

These were crucial times for the Santuario de Guadalupe and the Foundation. Gonzales tells it best here and in the next three chapters:

In 1975, the restoration project was chosen as the (lead) project for the nation's Bicentennial, which would be celebrated in 1976. At that time, the Foundation received money from the Federal government, the State of New Mexico and the City of Santa Fe. The original work was started in 1975, and the Santuario was reopened to the public as a performing arts and museum center on December 12, 1976.

The Foundation took care of various assignments, such as trying to raise more money as the original grants—more than $400,000—were spent on the crumbling edifice. In 1977, I was asked by Father Leo Lucero (pastor of the Guadalupe Parish) and Foundation member Michael Branch to join the board. Father Lucero was concerned that perhaps (the focus of) Foundation had become too secular (although that was the purpose of the Archdiocese handing over the Santuario to the Foundation, which would seek public funds on behalf of and serve the entire Santa Fe community—including Roman

Catholics, Protestants, Jews, other faiths and non-believers, Hispanics, Indians and Anglos; the Foundation had exceeded these goals beyond measure early on, but change was in the wind).

I accepted the invitation and joined the Foundation board in 1978. Gabrielle Palmer, the co-founding member of the Foundation (with Father Lucero) stepped down as director of the Foundation in 1979 and was succeeded by Jose Griego de Maestras.

In 1980, a new, more conservative (religiously oriented) board was in charge of the Foundation, and the first edition of what became the Foundation's newsletter, *La Noticias de Santiago de Guadalupe*, was published. During the four years I was on the board the first time (1978–84), fellow board member Jim Meeker donated a Yamaha Grand Piano to the Santuario. What a glorious gift!

Director Griego y Maestas subsequently resigned in 1981 and was succeeded by Virginia Castellano, who came highly recommended by those who knew and had worked with her previously. At about that time, however, I had served my four-year term on the board and felt the need of a break. It may have been a volunteer job, but I've never worked so hard in my life!

When 1984 rolled around, Father Lucero told me the board had not been meeting regularly as we used to do and were supposed to do according to our bylaws. He suggested that I might be able to help get things going again. I could not say no to him or the challenge.

That challenge included a financial shortfall of serious proportions. The FICA taxes for our one employee, the director, had not been paid. The Federal government, in turn, filed a lien against the Foundation for $5,000 of back employment taxes, plus penalties and interest, totaling more than $10,000. Fund-raising became the board's first and foremost effort at this time, thus giving rise to a new program: 'Our Lady Needs Help,' and both the board and community responded positively.

One of the first things we did was to confer with Edmundo Delgado, who suggested we contact Mountain Bell, the local telephone company. Delgado noted that the company had a 'community involvement team' that could be helpful to the Foundation. Thus, Mountain Bell, part of the nationwide Bell

Telephone system, helped organize the first of what would become an annual rummage sale on behalf of the Santuario on the company's lot off Sawmill Road in 1985.

In 1986, board members Antonio Portaga and Jim Meeker contributed a total of $4,000. This was like a shot in the arm and helped raise awareness of the financial need by the board.

Mountain Bell, in the person of the company's president, George Gillespie, came through again in 1987 with a much-needed donation. At that point, another angel appeared in the form of Baca Electric, which donated lightening rods that would draw lightening strikes away from the building. Steps had to be taken one at a time, to ensure the stability of both the Santuario and the Foundation.

The first of many small miracles occurred when Ray Latham said to Director Castellano: 'I think you need a good sign in front of the (Santuario).' At the time, the only sign on the property was a 4x8-foot sheet of plywood that had been painted white and hand-lettered, Santuario de Guadalupe, by the first director years ago.

Latham said he could create professional signage at his own expense. The board jumped at the offer, and he went to work. Within several months, Latham reappeared with the beautiful sign that still stands today.

Ray Latham designed and built this sign in the mid 1980s that still stands in front of the Santuario today. Photograph by Edward Gonzales.

Suggesting a retail cost of $16,000, Latham donated the sign: In the center (is) a carving of Our Lady of Guadalupe, with raised lettering 'Santuario de Nuestra Senora de Guadalupe' and a circle on the bottom of the sign acknowledging the Guadalupe Historic Foundation. (Be sure to take note of this work of art when you pass by the Santuario; it's on the southeast corner of the property in front of the Santuario.)

With the new sign in place, our (financial) luck began to change in 1987. The Santa Fe Desert Chorale, founded by and under the direction of Lawrence Bandfield, began producing their summer programs at the Santuario. Edmundo Delgado came through for the Santuario again when he proposed an idea that would involve the city's business community on an on-going basis.

Delgado would organize entertainment activities and events that would appeal to the community at large and enlist the companies as sponsors of the particular events. The merchant could sell and/or give tickets to patrons at no expense to the Foundation that, in turn, received a set amount for the use of the Santuario.

The first of these events was a concert by classical guitarist, Craig Dell, followed by a satire play (about) the mythical figure, Dona Tules, by Van Ann Moore. At about the same time (late '80s), the Foundation sponsored the first Las Posadas, in conjunction with the Santa Fe Chamber of Commerce. It was held at Rancho Encantado, north of Tesuque, with the site donated by the owner, Betty Egan. The Foundation paid for the catering and decorations, including farolitos and luminarias. More than 300 people paid $25 each for a reception, light dinner and the historic procession. This was the first of many Las Posadas sponsored by the Guadalupe Historic Foundation.

Closing out the year (1987) was a lovely two-day program put on by the then-College of Santa Fe and the Foundation looking to the future: 'Guadalupe '88'.

The New Year saw more shows co-sponsored with the business community, which raised various amounts of money. Edmundo Delgado brought in many wonderful artists who, in turn, drew many community members to the Santuario, many of whom had never seen the beautiful interior of the little chapel...that soon would need serious improvements.

In the meantime, the Foundation board welcomed new members: Ambassador Frank Ortiz, Ed Berry and Ray Herrera, who noted that the Cathedral was (and is) his parish, but his heart belonged—and still does—to the Santuario. During this time, Lorraine Goldman succeeded Virginia Castellano as director. Goldman was particularly good at working with the media and producing material about the Santuario for the general public.

With the help of Ambassador Ortiz, the interest and penalties that had accrued to the back taxes were eliminated, and the Foundation board was able—thanks to a low-interest loan from First National Bank of Santa Fe—to pay off the $5,000 owed in FICA taxes. (Among the bank's owners at the time was a Spanish corporation. A coincidence? Perhaps...or, maybe, it was another one of those miracles!)

One thing after another occurred to the Santuario and required attention during this time. For instance, the bell tower began leaking and starting to lean toward the eastern side of the Santuario. In fact, during one of the Desert Chorale summer concerts in 1988, a rainstorm hit the City and water began to leak down from the bell tower and onto a box of concert programs set up along the east wall.

Desert Chorale Director Bandfield apologized profusely to the audience and asked if there was anyone who either was, or might know someone, able to donate money to help fix the roof. It would take a while, but another small miracle would occur down the road.

The board could not wait, however, and began repairs with money already in the coffers. Local archeologist and contractor Ed Crocker was hired to patch the roof. With a team of laborers, he lifted the tin roofing that had come loose over the years and, with chalking guns, he shot tar into the open space to close off the leaky areas.

Still, the bell tower was in need of repair. With the roof fixed, at least temporarily, I noticed there was a pipe sticking out of the north side of the bell tower. Checking with Crocker whether that pipe was a drainpipe, he said there was no pipe visible when you were looking down from the top of the tower.

Apparently, the pipe was closed off and tarred over during the restoration in the '70s, creating a small pool. So, every time it rained or snowed, the water collected and eventually the leak was created. The pool would dry up when the weather was dry but would fill up when the monsoons and snowstorms hit the area, resulting in leaking down the east wall into the Santuario.

Measurements were taken, and it was discovered the bell tower already had moved easterly by about one-half-to-three-quarters of an inch. We knew we were in trouble, and it could only get worse.

Then, another one of those miracles occurred, one that ultimately would backfire but saved the day in the meantime.

2

The Plug is Pulled

The tumultuous year of 1988 was drawing to a close when, miracle of miracles, a couple from Chicago, Jean and Joseph Sullivan, came to the Foundation board of directors offering $200,000 to replace the bell tower. They had read about the Santuario's plight in a Roman Catholic publication and wanted to help.

The board was so excited at the time and turned to Foundation cofounder and board member, Father Leo Lucero, to direct the project. By that time, Father Leo had been transferred from pastor of Our Lady of Guadalupe parish to head of the parish of Cristo Rey in Santa Fe. He continued his faith and efforts on behalf of the Santuario.

The offer of $200,000 particularly was exciting, because it was the single largest grant since the original monies collected early on. Perhaps this clouded the board's judgment, as it voted overwhelmingly to accept the Sullivan's offer. One of our members, however, cast a more jaundiced eye. Felice Gonzales, a lawyer and the board's legal council, noted the many 'strings' attached to the offer and urged caution. For instance, she said, the deadlines to accomplish certain tasks might be onerous to meet—and, the terms of the grant demanded compliance with the strict time frame.

Felice was right. The board began the work on the bell tower project right around Christmas, when the agreement finally was signed. Everyone was busy with the holiday and happy to have the necessary work under way.

Concerned with other things at the time, the board members were a little lax in meeting the terms of the contract. Father Leo plunged right in and began the required arduous task of translating various psalms for the benefit of everyone in Santa Fe; this included presenting said psalms in Spanish, English and several Indian languages, including Tewa and Kerese.

After the holidays, Mrs. Sullivan returned from her home in Chicago to inspect our progress and pronounced her disappointment with the fact that the bell tower was still standing, the destruction of which was among other things called for in the grant. The board tried to explain that the first order of business was hiring a structural engineer to determine what exactly needed to be done, and this hiring had been accomplished and the engineer, indeed, was at work on said determination.

The old tower was built of brick atop adobe walls, and this proved to be a conflict of the two different materials used on the church in earlier restorations. For instance, parts of the outside walls that did not face inclement weather were plastered with mud, while those areas that would be most affected by adverse weather elements were plastered with stucco. This produced a big contrast in appearance, especially when the elements began wearing the materials. So, the board determined that the surrounding walls should be dealt with before the bell tower itself.

Mrs. Sullivan could see only the deadlines for various aspects of the restoration, and the first of these was the tower itself. With $50,000 of the grant in hand, the board agreed to do a list of things she imposed before her next visit in February. This list was completed but, once again, the old bell tower stood, waiting for the structural engineer's report. The engineer met with both Sullivans during this time and explained the need to secure the old tower first, suggesting that it would not be necessary to tear it down and construct a new tower that would be far more expensive and unnecessary.

The Sullivans, much to everyone's relief, agreed to this determination, so a contract for the new plan was drawn up. Much to the chagrin of the board, the Sullivans had demanded that any type of work on the tower had to be forwarded to and approved by them. Once again, the board members in their haste took little note of this stipulation and began the work deemed necessary by the engineer.

The work began from the bottom up, necessitating the removal of the flooring at the east end of the Santuario that supported the bell tower. Upon removing the old flooring, a mass grave including numerous burials was found underneath. The aforementioned Ed Crocker, a contractor and archaeologist, was involved with the project and, on his own, felt the need to notify the local media at the same time he informed the Foundation board of the grave's existence. The board subsequently learned that in New Mexico such burial sites required state examination before work could proceed. Thus, work on the area underneath the tower stopped immediately, as the press reported.

Unfortunately, the Sullivans learned of this situation through the media and were very disturbed by it. They felt they should have been contacted first, before even the state was informed and certainly before the general public might read about it in their hometown newspaper.

This brought an immediate visit from the Sullivans, who informed the board of trustees that they, indeed, were in breach of contract and subject to a lawsuit, not to mention that no further monies would be available. Finally, the board realized that the Sullivans really wanted to micro-manage the entire project, from afar, with the board only to do what they wanted done. This, as Felice Gonzales had predicted, was unacceptable.

Thus, the board did what it had to do: the contract was rescinded, with the original $50,000 to be returned to the Sullivans in installments. The latter would take time, but the Foundation board was determined that its hands could not be tied any longer. In the meantime, the bell tower stabilization was completed, as promised, and required quite an engineering feat. Despite the haste, that tower still stands in good shape.

The Sullivans finally agreed to the contract termination and told the board that it would not be necessary to return the initial $50,000 because they had filed their income taxes for 1988 (when the money was given to the Foundation), and it would be more costly to them to file an amendment than to take the money back. It seems rather mundane to consider such details but, as noted, the Sullivans were most concerned with details.

It should be pointed out here that, as mentioned above, state officials were informed of the grave under the flooring on the east end of the Santuario—in front of the main door to the structure—and an investigation and study of the site ensued. In that connection, experts from the University of New Mexico examined the bones to determine when and why they were put there. The authorities particularly were concerned whether these people might have died of disease or mass illness.

Both the Archdiocese and the Foundation Board agreed to the research project. It was found that the gravesite contained a total of 63 remains, including 46 individuals ranging in age from toddler to mature adult of Hispanic, Anglo, Indian and African-American origin, dating back to the mid-18th century. While the examination produced these numbers, it could not pin down how or why the remains wound up where they did.

The bones were respectfully blessed and placed in a crypt built by the Foundation under the new flooring where they had been found. The remains had been placed in more than 70 small boxes, which were interred in a crypt made of four-foot-by-eight-foot, one-quarter-inch steel plate and lined with wood. Father Leo performed the interment ceremony in the Santuario.

Father Leo Lucero blesses human remains reinterred after discovery during renovation of the Santuario de Guadalupe, Santa Fe, New Mexico, 1989. Courtesy of the Palace of the Governors Photo Archives (NMHM/DCA), HP.2014.14.1408. (From *The Santa Fe New Mexican* Collection. Photograph by Leslie Tallant.)

3

An Angel Appears

*T*he local media in Santa Fe covered the archeological study exten-sively. Many visitors to the City Different would subscribe to *The Santa Fe New Mexican* upon their return home. One such visitor, John Herklotz of California, did just that and read the paper closely in 1989.

Herklotz had a more personal and professional reason for his interest in Santa Fe and its daily newspaper: His company—Cellular Financial Corp of Pacific Palisades, California—had just been awarded a Federal Communi-cations Commission contract for cellular phone service in nine New Mexico counties, including Santa Fe County. He wanted to keep track of local reaction to the contract and measure its progress.

When he read the story, Herklotz placed a call to the Santuario. Edward Gonzales said. "I happened to be there at the time and took the call. It proved to be both providence and a blessing for the Santuario. Noting that he was coming to Santa Fe the next day, Herklotz said he would like to meet with me and discuss financial concerns and the future of the Santuario.

Herklotz told me, 'When you do business in a community, you want to provide something in return. (The Santuario) is an important part of Santa Fe. It's been here 200 years, and I'd like to see it here for another 200 years.' He also was a film producer in Hollywood, through Herklotz Enterprises, Inc.

We talked over lunch the day of his arrival, during which he proposed to give the Foundation a matching grant of $100,000, with the proviso that the organization would have to raise another $100,000. Herklotz added that we could raise the money any way we chose. This included rental of the non-sectarian Santuario for art and music presentations, donations from other individuals and/or groups and the sale of any items (such as posters depicting Our Lady of Guadalupe) and services.

With that offer, the Foundation's board of trustees hustled and put together an extensive program. We had a fund-raiser in honor of one of our members—Concha Ortiz y Pino de Kleven—that produced $6,000 for the effort, plus another $6,000 from a dear friend of hers who also supported the Santuario. We also had a $5,000 donation from Farther Crispin Butz on behalf of St. Francis Cathedral. With multitudinous smaller donations, it added up and we achieved the $100,000 matching grant. As promised, Herklotz contributed his $100,000 and we went to work over the ensuing six-to-seven years.

Our first major project involved the water-soaked outside walls of the Santuario. The Foundation board hired Gilbert Duran, owner of P.C.I. Construction, to change the style of the outside fire walls back to the California mission style and plaster them accordingly. He suggested, and the board agreed, that a cement plaster be applied, both for longevity and maintenance. He proceeded to set up extensive scaffolding, which had to meet strict federal standards. The plastering job was about to begin, when the Archdiocese Committee of Historical Preservation objected to the plastering method—the Committee wanted the plaster to be lime adobe mud, not adobe cement—and ordered the scaffolding taken down.

We found ourselves in this predicament because after the Sullivan's grant debacle, the Foundation board had approached the Archdiocese about taking back the deed to the Santuario and surrounding land for financial and legal protection. Thus, the Santuario was re-deeded from the Guadalupe Historic Foundation to the Archdiocese in 1991...with the stipulations that the Foundation would continue to direct the daily operations of the Santuario for the next 15 years and the Archdiocese would have final approval on any major changes to or for the Santuario during that time.

We (the board) assumed continuing repair and update of the building itself fell within the purview of the board and did not require review by and approval of the Archdiocese. The latter disagreed, strongly. After much debate and study, all of which was covered by the local media, the cement-based plastering once again was ordered, new scaffolding erected and work was completed in 1992.

Duran and P.C.I. construction also put on a sorely needed new roof in '92. It, too, was a replica of the 1922 roof, including new tin tiles produced by the same company in St. Louis that had done the earlier roof. With this effort, the Santuario and Sacristy were covered.

In 1993, Ray Herrera, one of our board members, led the effort to install new flooring in the Santuario, as well as a new threshold on the front door, which had been vandalized in a bungled burglary attempt. Ray was active in the local labor movement and went to members of the carpenter's union for help with replacing the flooring. With a load of lumber donated by the Alpine Lumber Co., the volunteer carpenters managed the job over a weekend. Ray, three of his brothers and cousins, and other board members—including myself—pitched in, as well.

With a brand new roof and floor, newly plastered and painted walls, the Santuario was the gem envisioned by the Foundation and its many members and volunteers.

The miracles continued in 1995-96 when two of our board members, Albuquerque residents Concha Ortiz y Pino de Kleven and George Pearl, decided to have lunch before a board meeting at the Hotel St. Francis. While lunching, George talked with Goodwin Taylor, the owner of the hotel, for whom he had been the architect when Taylor converted what had been the Hotel DeVargas into the Hotel St. Francis.

George told Taylor about the altar paining of the Virgin of Guadalupe by Jose de Alzibar in 1783, noting that it was in need of continuing preservation. Experts from the National Historic Society cited the painting as one of the five most significant paintings in the United States and required a proper environment to preserve it. This included air conditioning for the hot summer months, something that we (the board) had talked about since 1991.

"Taylor happened to be an air-conditioning specialist, and George asked him to come to the Santuario and assess the situation. Taylor agreed, and I gave him an extensive tour of the Santuario, including the area between the eves and into the bell tower. Taylor said he thought air conditioning units could be installed very easily and simply.

He said he was planning to order a multiple unit for the new Las Campanas community clubhouse and, lo and behold, a month later, Taylor told me: 'I have a present for you people. I got the manufacturer to donate a unit for the Santuario.' Taylor proceeded to enlist Bradbury & Stamm Construction Co., based in Albuquerque, to bring a crane and lift one unit in the bell tower and the other on the floor in the north side of the building. Thanks to Taylor, installation of the cooling system was donated by a local contractor, Cliff Crouch, who owned the Carrier Air Conditioning franchise. Ultimately, the Santuario received a $250,000 air-conditioning system and $500,000 installation for free. Such a miracle!

Other improvements included fixing the drainage in the entry way and surrounding brick area, as well as the installation of lighted steps up to the Santuario from the parking lot below. We also raised $16,000 during this period that was earmarked for a new handicap ramp, which was installed, and a handicapped-based rest room, which was not.

Once again, however, problems—in the person of a new parish priest— were on the horizon.

4

The Troubles Begin and End

While celebrating each and every small miracle that came our (Foundation's) way, we held a board meeting the day after Fiesta in September. It was then that we learned that the Guadalupe parish had been assigned a new priest: Father Bill Sanchez. Most of the board members knew Father Bill's Mother and Dad, because they had been very active in the Santa Fe community for many years.

So, we saw Father Bill's appointment as a cause for celebration. It didn't last long.

At our request, Director Gabby Ortiz invited him to join us that day. Father Bill arrived with what he said were instructions from the Archbishop (Michael Sheehan) to turn the Santuario into a place for perpetual adoration. This would mean no community activities, such as art shows, musical presentations and other events that would raise much-needed funds to maintain the Santuario.

We, as a foundation board, were not prepared to acquiesce to this alleged request/demand from the Archbishop, and we told Father Bill that. If, in fact, the Archbishop wanted to take over the role of the Santuario, the Archdiocese would need to pick up all the expenses—approximately $52,000 annually—that would include insurance, maintenance, daily operations and salary for the director, things that the Foundation covered through fund-raising events, as well as civil grants and donations (that were tax-deductible to the donors, because the Foundation was a not-for-profit corporation).

Father Bill responded that he didn't know what the Archbishop had in mind in terms of financial arrangements but would check and get back to us. We noted that an additional cost would be in providing for security if the Santuario was to be open at night in perpetual adoration. (When we had nighttime events, the director and volunteers would maintain security.) Father Bill and, according to him, the Archbishop, had not considered these things before he approached the Foundation board.

Of immediate concern, and needing a response right away, was a request from former Santa Fe Mayor and businessman Joe Valdes to use the Santuario for his wedding reception. (Mayor Valdes had secured a grant from the federal Model Cities program in 1976 to help with the initial restoration of the Santuario under the direction of the newly formed Guadalupe Historic Foundation. He subsequently became a widower and planned to remarry in '97, with the night wedding to be performed at St. Francis Cathedral, followed by a small, private reception at the Santuario.)

We (the board) agreed to his request, considering all that Mayor Valdes had done for the Santuario and Santa Fe community. There was to be no liquor at the reception, other than a single Champagne toast to the bride and groom at the end of the reception. I feel the need to point this out, because others accused the Foundation of allowing liquor throughout the reception.

During the reception, Father Bill and a visiting priest from Arizona came into the Santuario uninvited and proceeded to stroll around, talking to the guests. No one objected at the time but, about a week later, a few Guadalupe Parish parishioners began a public protest during already scheduled programs at the Santuario. We, the board members, were not informed of these plans, until Father Bill and the parishioners—who called themselves Los Hermanos Cruzados—showed up at the next event. We, as an all-volunteer board who sought and relied upon community support, felt ambushed. Subsequently, the group would march around and hassle the folks attending each event.

In the meantime, Father Bill never talked directly to the Foundation board again. Finally, after a month of harassment by Father Bill and Los

Hermanos Cruzados, the board contacted Archbishop Sheehan, requesting an audience with him and Father Bill. We particularly wanted Father Bill to explain to the Archbishop what he was doing and why at the Santuario.

The audience was granted, and Foundation President Don Ortiz and I joined Father Bill and a few other members of the Guadalupe Parish at the meeting in Albuquerque. Other priests from the diocese came to the meeting, as well. Archbishop Sheehan asked Father Bill just what his intentions were, since he (the Archbishop) had not given him any instructions as to the operation of the Santuario. The Archbishop also wanted to know just how far Father Bill planned to take the protest.

These questions were not answered, neither while we were there nor subsequently. (Presumably, the others in attendance at the meeting met privately. We, Don Ortiz and I, were not invited to participate in that gathering.) So, things in Santa Fe stayed the same, with Father Bill and his little group of protestors continually harassing the Foundation board, the Santuario director and those attending the various events.

The protest continued for seven months, during which our poor director (Gabby Ortiz) became so upset that his health declined. After all, he was on the front line at all the Santuario's events, welcoming visitors and attendees and trying to handle the protestors, who became more bold and demanding over time.

These events were covered in the local media extensively; in fact, the *Albuquerque Journal* gave almost daily coverage—most of it, from Father Bill's perspective. The daily *Santa Fe New Mexican* and weekly *Santa Fe Reporter* usually were more even-handed. Once the general public became aware, through the media, of what was going on, we board members began to get a lot of flack and were accused of all kinds of things.

We found it very difficult to defend ourselves without getting the Church involved, but we did it as best we could. Then, after seven months, Archbishop gave Father Bill an ultimatum: 'Either accept a transfer (to Mountainair, New Mexico) or be defrocked,' which meant he no longer would be a priest in the Roman Catholic Church. Father Bill accepted the transfer and is yet a priest in New Mexico.

A new priest, the Reverend Michael Shea, came to Guadalupe Parish, and we found we usually could work with him when it came to the Santuario. We (the board) invited Father Shea to the Santuario to conduct weekday Masses; unfortunately, we discovered after the fact that he had twice forgotten to lock the Santuario when the Masses ended and people departed. Vagrants got in, and the Santuario was upset by their presence.

Fearing serious vandalism over time, the board informed Father Shea that the arrangement (wherein he would accept responsibility for security by both unlocking and then locking the Santuario) was not working out. The open-door policy had to end. Parish members once again got on their high horses (although none of them offered to either pay for or provide such security) and protested.

As time went on, a Foundation board member who worked for the Archdiocese said the Archbishop had told her he wanted the Santuario back under his wing, expenses and all, and would not renew the lease with the Foundation that had almost five years to go at that point. Because I saw no future for the Guadalupe Historic Foundation and certainly not my role, I withdrew and ended my membership on the board in late 2001.

It haunts me to this day, however, that there were and are those in the Guadalupe Parish and the Santa Fe Community who act in what I would call an unchristian way and still accuse the Foundation and its board of negative things that never occurred. Most, if not all, of these accusations come from people who were not present at any of the criticized activities and relied on hearsay and innuendo.

I want the story to be rectified, because we never knowingly did anything wrong and certainly tried to act in the best interests of the Santuario of Our Lady and the people of Santa Fe over the years. Perhaps the only thing we did wrong was that we did too good a job! Once the various restorations had been completed and the Santuario was in good shape, both structurally and financially, the Archdiocese wanted it back. (Ultimately, the Foundation continued to manage the Santuario until it was fully returned to the Archdiocese in early 2006.)

The Santuario was and is a result of many miracles, both big and small. If it weren't for Our Lady guiding us throughout the years, none of the successes would have been possible. She led us (the Foundation and its many dedicated volunteers over the years) through trials and tribulations that most people would not have accepted, and we could not have done so without Her.

Interior of the Santuario de Guadalupe as it appears today.

5

The Past as Prologue

*T*he following vignettes highlight the people and events that capture the essence of the Guadalupe Historic Foundation's work and the many people—all volunteers—who saved and preserved the Santuario de Guadalupe for generations to come. They labored mostly in silence and behind the scenes; here, we bring them forward and shine a light on their devotion and accomplishments.

Vignette 1

Dolores (Dee Dee) Myers, a congregant of the Santuario de Guadalupe, and her family were instrumental in the maintenance of the Santuario in the early 1970s—before the massive restoration in the mid-1970s—and restoration of the 1783 Jose de Alzibar painting by Dr. Elstela Rodriquez Cubero of Paraguay. Courtesy of the family.

Before the Foundation was created in 1975–76, members of the Guadalupe Parish and Santa Fe community were concerned about and sought to improve both the condition and future of the Santuario. Dolores Quintana Myers (1935–2014) was one of those people.

Dolores was born and raised just down the street from the Santuario, where she attended school through the eight grade. It was said she grew to love the Guadalupe parish, which enveloped her, and the Racine Dominican nuns who gave her a splendid basic education.

As time went on, and a new church was built in 1961, the Santuario fell into serious disrepair. By 1969, it was closed to the public, while homeless individuals found refuge at night by entering through broken windows and rotting doors. The pipes from the organ were pulled out, bent and broken until it finally was sold as scrap. Perhaps the worst and most noticeable thing was the 1783 Jose de Alzibar painting, which had begun to fall apart. (It originally was executed in 20 separate pieces.)

Dolores took it upon herself to ask a priest who formerly had been assigned to the Guadalupe parish to return to the Santuario and advise her on what could be done. He, unfortunately, said the Archdiocese could not help because of a lack of funds and direction, adding that it would be up to parishioners such as she to do what they could.

Discouraged but unbowed, Dolores approached the Paraguayan artist who had done artistic restorations at Cristo Rey Church on Canyon Road. Dr. Estela Rodriquez Cubero visited the Santuario and was dismayed at its condition and that of the painting, commenting that the condition of both was "disgraceful."

At first, Dr. Rodriquez said she could not help but urged Dolores to find those who would. Then, a small miracle occurred when the artist said she would stay...if the parish would provide money for her time, a place to live, sustenance and the equipment necessary to repair the painting, as well as a clean place to do the work.

Dolores went into high gear, calling upon the Parish Council (of which she was a member) to meet in special session. While Council members echoed the words of the priest before, they encouraged Dolores and others to continue with the project and provide the necessary ingredients for Dr.

Rodriquez Cubero to perform the work themselves. Fund-raising efforts began the next day; plus, housing was provided for the artist and a carpenter secured to make a new frame and construct a new front door. Then, they went to work and cleaned the entire interior of the Santuario.

Interested friends and parishioners would come by to watch Dr. Rodriquez work and to share their stories and experience in the Santuario over the years. This provided even greater motivation and determination, and the day of the hanging of the repaired and cleaned painting was proclaimed.

The church was cleaned, windows repaired and the outside walls newly plastered. A bank loan was needed to help pay for all this and was signed by several Guadalupe parishioners, but it was Dolores who paid off the entire loan. Then, interest in the Santuario began to grow in the community, from a local museum director to the Chancery office.

The local team of working parishioners was replaced by folks who ultimately created the Guadalupe Historic Foundation. Dolores was pleased to step down; she and her little band of parishioners, including her family, had accomplished their goals. They had saved the Santuario, handing it over to a Foundation that would flourish for the next 30 years.

Make no mistake: it was Dolores Quintana Myers' dream and hard work, plus her faith in Our Lady de Guadalupe, which made all this happen. She believed and proved that one person could make a difference.

Vignette 2

Young people played an important role in the early years of restoration, too. The Guadalupe Parish youth group determined in the summer of 1972 that its members would manage the St. Vincent de Paul clothing and household furnishings distribution. The storage area was in the office behind, and connected to, the Santuario that, once again, had fallen into disuse.

The youngsters were given access to the Santuario, as well as the office where they worked. Curious about the Santuario, the kids were dismayed to find the old church inhabited by pigeons and reportedly at least one vagrant who made his home in the choir loft.

St. Vincent de Paul was set aside for the moment as the young people rounded up brooms for the dirt and shovels to remove the human and pigeon excrement. One young man said at the time: "It was terrible. It took us two whole weekends to clean out the place." A young woman echoed him, saying "I spent more time cleaning the Santuario than I did my bedroom, and it was a mess, too!"

The following Sunday, they celebrated their work with a candlelight mass in the Santuario. The youth mass featured guitars and song, as well as prayer.

The youngsters watched over the church during the remaining weeks of that summer, until the caring adults returned in the fall.

Vignette 3

While Our Lady of Guadalupe has long been considered a miracle, the term was used in reference to the Santuario de Guadalupe itself by Foundation President Antonio de Pedro in March, 1991. Used in this reference, it first appeared in print in the July, 1991, Foundation minutes when noted Marian scholar, Jacqueline Dunnington, quoted President de Pedro and suggested the restored Santuario itself was the result of a miraculous challenge issued by the Santa Fe community and accepted by the Guadalupe Historic Foundation.

Vignette 4

Jacqueline Dunnington had become involved, as an observer, with the Santuario and Foundation in the fall of 1985, when she was a guest of the Foundation at its September board meeting. She and Martin Kelly, a local lawyer, businessman and self-described "devotee of Our Lady," proposed a memorial pilgrimage at the Santuario for the annual Feast Day, December 12. They viewed such an event as an educational and cultural activity for the community.

Jacqueline Dunnington continued her interest in and support of the Foundation and the Santuario by writing extensively on the history of Our

Lady of Guadalupe and the Santuario, proclaiming the Santuario de Guadalupe "the oldest continuously standing shrine to Our Lady of Guadalupe in
the United States." She also designed note cards with Our Lady of Guadalupe
motif, with all proceeds going to the Foundation.

Vignette 5

Among the earliest and most hands-on volunteers was Dorothy Wade,
who, along with the Casa Alegre Garden Club, restored the Bicentennial
Heritage Garden planted on the south side of the Santuario by Cordelia Hall
in 1976 and went on to create the award-winning Plants of the Holy Land in
1984.

Dorothy Wade continued her efforts on beautifying the property
surrounding the Santuario and was lauded by the weekly Santa Fe Reporter,
calling her the "fairy godmother" of the Santuario gardens in April, 1988. The
Casa Alegre Garden Club continued maintaining the gardens after Wade's
retirement in 1989.

Vignette 6

Robert McKinney, long-time publisher of The Santa Fe New Mexican,
and his wife, Marielle, donated two exquisite religious paintings to the Santuario in 1979, with the proviso that they always would be displayed in the
Santuario. Years later, the McKinneys agreed that the Santuario could use the
paintings in any way the Foundation decreed. At the close of the Foundation
in January, 2006, the paintings were given to the Archdiocese of Santa Fe and
reside in the archives.

Well before that, in 1975, soon after the Foundation was created,
the McKinneys introduced architect Nathaniel Owings to the Foundation
board members, who accepted his suggestions to employ contractors Victor
Johnson and Robert Nestor to handle the restoration. While studying the
Santuario, they discovered an original lintel (a rendering of which became
the motif of the Foundation's logo) and restored it. It was decided that "the

best course of action" would be to return the Santuario to its original 18th century appearance. (They were able to restore the interior of the Santuario before the funding ran out. It was left to future Foundation board members to both undertake the exterior restoration and raise the money for it.)

Significant workers on the initial restoration project included Danny Porter, the major contractor; Jonathan Huntress, who worked on restoring the windows; and Thayer Carter, Frank Turley and Hans Wright, all master craftsmen. "We finally found the 18th century church...and, it was beautiful," said Gabrielle Palmer, a founder and original Foundation board member.

Vignette 7

In 1988, an Architectural Advisory Committee was initiated to tackle the long-awaited exterior restoration. The committee's membership included Edward Archuleta, chair and a member of the Foundation board; Sam Baca, New Mexico Community Foundation/Churches Project; Victor Johnson, Johnson-Nestor Architects; Terry Morgart, National Park Service exhibits specialist; Dr. Gabrielle Palmer, historian and co-founder of the Guadalupe Historic Foundation; Beverly Spears, architect; Mike Taylor, Museum of New Mexico Monuments Unit; and Barbara Zook, State Historic Preservation Division.

By 1990, the board had chosen restoration architect Guadalupe Castillo and agreed that the exterior of the Santuario should be restored to the 1920s California Mission style. (The Santuario had been cited in the 1020s as "a significant structure within the Historic District" of Santa Fe by the National Register of Historic Sites. It also was listed in the State Register of Cultural Properties during that time.)

Additionally, the Santa Fe Archdiocese Commission for the Preservation of Historic New Mexico Churches and the State Historic Preservation Division of the State Office of Cultural Affairs signed off on the restoration project.

Vignette 8

Local artisans built and donated various accessories to the Santuario. They included Ray Latham, who produced the main sign in front of the Santuario that still stands today, as well as guide signs for the Santuario in 1988. In early 1979, Luis Tapia gave two wooden benches to the Santuario in 1979. Jim Meeker donated a much-needed answering machine and loaned the piano that resonated with the outstanding acoustics in the Santuario and subsequently used by various performers and groups, including the Desert Chorale.

Donated time and effort came in various guises during the 1980s. They included the translation of interpretive material into Spanish by Sam Adelo, votive candle holders donated by Becky Archuleta and Rosina Escudero, managing the Santuario by Ed Archuleta, typewriter repair by Mike Branch, photography by Peter Dechert, brass candlesticks from De Pedro International, drip irrigation system installation by George Gillespie and Paul Spangle, legal services (for the Foundation) by Felice Gonzales and Bryant Rogers, informational tape/English by Mike Langer, typesetting by Steven Lowe of Casa Sin Nombre, painting of the cross above the Santuario by Willie Lynch and Luis Perea (who climbed atop the cross to accomplish the work), event ticket sales by Jo McCrossen, computer services by Bill McGonigle, preparation of the mailing list by Linder Meaders, handicap parking signs by the State Highway Department, refreshments at events offered by Our Lady of Guadalupe Altar Society and our Lady of Guadalupe ladies Society, calligraphy by Orlando Padilla, German translations by Karl-Heinz Planitz, accounting services by Norman Sackett, landscaping work by the Santa Fe Neighborhood Housing Services, graphics by Lou Frosh and David Smith, State Highway Marker by Robert Torres and Spanish informational tape by Sabine Ulibarri.

Volunteers also served as guides for visitors wishing to learn more about Our Lady and the Santuario. They included Pauline Brown, Milo and Will Hamilton, Bernadine Hesch, Patty Johnston, Irene B. de Martinez, Lucille McCulloch, Sarah Richardson, Dorothea and Clare Tallman, Gene Doty, Pete Trujillo, Frances Vieira and Charlotte White.

Office work was volunteered by Eutilia Alarid, Pauline Brown, Robin Carlson, Bernadine Hesch, Pete Trujillo and Charlotte White.

Vignette 9

Still others donated their time and energy to repair and restore the Santuario over the years, including Gilbert and Pauline Duran of PCI Contractors, Inc., restoration architect Guadalupe Castillo, Carpenters Union member Tom Olivas and 10 aspiring students, as well as Eddie Baca of Baca Lighting Protection and Polo Gomez, who contributed the bell for the restoration.

Vignette 10

Fund-raising was a constant concern and effort by the Foundation for the Santuario. There were notable community members who came forward when the Santuario was in need. Following is a list, surely not complete, of some of those individuals:

Actress Van Ann Moore presented her one-woman show, " A Historical Characterization," in which she portrayed Susan Shelby Magoffin, the first Anglo woman to come to Santa Fe via the Santa Fe Trail, and Maria Gertrudes Barcelo, aka Dona Tules Barcelo, Santa Fe's gambling proprietress, in November of 1987.

Margaret (Betty) Frosh and Jack Sears, who contacted foundations and businesses.

Lou Frosh, graphics editor, who designed and created the graphics for the Foundation's 1988 annual report.

Natalie Owings, daughter of architect Nathaniel Owings, who drew the original Santuario corbel, which became the motif for the Foundation's logo.

Artist Tony Eubank created a limited edition of prints depicting the 1890s' painting, "Santuario de Guadalupe," featuring parishioners walking to the Santuario for Christmas Eve Mass, with proceeds to go to the Foundation in 1996. The project was commissioned by Southwest Bank of Santa Fe.

Concha Ortiz y Pino de Kleven was a longtime supporter of both the Santuario de Guadalupe and the Guadalupe Historic Foundation, serving on the Foundation board and hosting fund-raising activities for the restoration and continue maintenance of the Santuario. Courtesy of the family.

Concha Ortiz y Pino de Kleven, who celebrated her birthday in 1990 with a fund-raiser for the Santuario. The effort drew both intimate friends and admirers who contributed generously on her behalf. (Concha also was a long-time member of the Foundation board and worked tirelessly on its behalf.)

Among the artists who showed at the Santuario were santero Charlie Carrillo, Dan Paulos, John Huckmala, Ellen Chavez de Litner, R. A. Gallegos, Frank Alarid, Jake Archuleta, Eric Werner, Bernardo C de Baca and James Cordova.

Musical presentations were given by Grimmel College; Baile Folklorico de Denver, Colorado; Santa Fe Stages production of Guadalupe; The Gay Men's Chorus of Albuquerque; Virginia Mackey (who celebrated her 100th birthday with a concert at the Santuario); Steel Point Theatre; Kammer Musik; the Waldorf Charter School Choir; Robin H. Bowen; the Holy Trinity Chorale; Serenata from Santa Fe; Santa Fe Music Conservatory; Santa Fe Women's Ensemble; Santa Fe Symphony; Coro de Camara; the Chesapeake Trio; and the Santa Fe Chamber Ensemble.

The Santa Fe Chamber Ensemble, whose members belonged to the Santa Fe Chamber Music Festival, performed in the Santuario de Guadalupe, Santa Fe, New Mexico, 1977. Courtesy of the Palace of the Governors Photo Archives (NMHM/DCA), HP.2014.14.568. (From *The Santa Fe New Mexican* Collection.)

Maria Benitez and the Institute for Spanish Arts made a special appearance at the Santuario in 1985, as did the Sangre de Cristo Chorale in 1987. For many years, the Sociedad Folklorica used the Santuario for its annual Merienda during Santa Fe Fiesta each September.

Other active fund-raisers on behalf of the Santuario were Eutilia Alarid, Craig Dell and George Gillespie.

The efforts of all of these folks benefited the Santuario for years to come; in fact, there is no end to the positive impact they—and others—have had over the years by their heartfelt contributions.

Vignette 11

Of special note were the financial contributions by John Herklotz, California businessman in the 1990s. (Please see Chapter 3 for details of his efforts on behalf of the Santuario de Guadalupe.) Besides being honored by the Guadalupe Historic Foundation, Herklotz was installed as a Knight of St. Gregory by Archbishop Michael Sheehan in 2000.

Vignette 12

Things were not always in perfect harmony among and within the Foundation board, its membership and the parish, despite good faith; in fact, there were bumps along the way often caused by a lack of communication or, almost worse, miscommunication. Even miracles have their setbacks, however temporary. Here are two that were faced, and overcome, by the Foundation on behalf of the Santuario with the help of Our Lady:

Gilbert Duran of PCI Contractors, Inc., first submitted a bid to perform restoration of the outside of the Santuario in February, 1991. It called for cement plaster and stucco, the then-current material of choice for both maintenance and protection of the structure. Subsequently, after the scaffolding had been erected and work was about to begin, Archdiocese officials demanded a soft lime-based plaster (that involved a lime, sand and water mixture) that they said was in keeping with religious structures.

The scaffolding came down, acrimony rose. Ultimately, Archbishop Robert Sanchez reversed the decision by his officials—after much study, discussion and threats of lawsuits—and ordered the Santuario be covered with cement plaster and stucco. The work was completed in the spring of 1992 and, the Santuario stands today. Duran and his company were honored by the Foundation board at later meetings.

The year 1997 saw protests at the Santuario when the new parish priest, Father Bill Sanchez, led a small group of parish members protesting what they saw as sacrilegious activities at the Santuario. These included art shows, musical presentations and, occasionally, receptions of one sort or another—all of which had been vetted by the Foundation board and the Archdiocese. They also felt the Santuario should be returned to the Archdiocese, which then would have to shoulder all the costs and expenses associated with a religious entity because grants no longer would be available from the federal, state or city governments, or other non-profit granting institutions. (It was noted that the parish and its parishioners never offered financial or volunteer help.)

These protests during such events upset artists and performers, as well as visitors, until finally, Archbishop Michael Sheehan ordered the protestors to cease and desist and then transferred 'Father Bill' to a parish in Mountainair, New Mexico.

In fact, the deed to the Santuario de Guadalupe had been transferred to the Archdiocese in early 1991, with the proviso that the Foundation would continue to both raise funds as a non-profit, secular entity and manage the daily activities of the Santuario. Under the terms of the new lease, as of February 1, 1991 and extending 25 years, the Archdiocese would be the lessor and the Foundation, the lessee. Then, each February 1, until 2006, the Foundation would pay the Archdiocese $1 for the privilege and responsibility of managing the Santuario. As of February 1, 2006, the Santuario de Guadalupe returned fully to the Archdiocese, where it resides to this day.

Vignette 13

At the same time, many organizations, all of them non-profit within the Santa Fe community, happily presented on-going programs on behalf of the Santuario over the years. Following are brief descriptions of two of them:

Las Posadas, which means lodging or accommodations, is a celebration stemming from Christian tradition and Spanish folklore. The one-night event features Mary and Joseph as they travel from Nazareth to Bethlehem, seeking lodging before Mary gives birth to Jesus. Many communities in Northern New Mexico follow this tradition, and Santa Fe is no exception. At each place the couple stops, the Devil appears and drives them away. At the end of their search, they find refuge in a stable.

In 1988, the Guadalupe Historic Foundation saw an opportunity to benefit both the community and the Foundation's coffers. At the same time, the owners of Rancho Encantado—Betty and John Egan—decided to keep the resort open during the winter, and they were looking for a fund-raiser for a yet-to-be determined local charity.

In a meeting of the minds, the Foundation board and the Egans began a 13-year tradition of presenting Las Posadas at Rancho Encantado. For a minimal fee (initially $25 per person, later raised to $30), visitors got a traditional Northern New Mexico dinner, with all the trimmings, mulled wine and the requisite pilgrimage. The Egans provided the facilities, a burro for the procession and all the wood for 20 luminarias.

The Foundation provided the persons portraying Mary and Joseph, their costumes, singers for Las Posadas, song books with Christmas carols and 500 farrolitos, as well as someone to fill the sacks and place them appropriately. More than 300 people attended that first Las Posadas at Rancho Encantado—many thanks to then-board member, Catherine Zacher, who was executive director of the Santa Fe Chamber of Commerce and posted a notice about the event in the Chamber newsletter to approximately 1,000 members—and the Foundation earned more than $5,000. The Egans were so enthusiastic that they suggested that the resort host the annual event (sponsored by the Guadalupe Historic Foundation), and so the resort did—even after Betty's death and John's subsequent retirement—through 2000.

One of the premier musical groups in Santa Fe, the Desert Chorale began a 13-year association with the Santuario in 1983. Led by Lawrence Bandfield, the Chorale performed its summer program and then holiday concerts at the Santuario. Bandfield said the building's acoustics were the best in the City Different, and he particularly appreciated the Yamaha Grand piano loaned to the Santuario by board member Jim Meeker.

Vignette 14

And, there was a significant celebration in 1998, when the Santuario hosted the inaugural event of the Cuarto (400) Centennial observance—a year-long celebration of the Spanish occupation of Santa Fe: "Ancient Kingdom of new Mexico and its Capital, Villa Real de Santa Fe." The Archdiocese, in the person of Father Jerome Martinez y Alire, recognized and commended two of the coordinators of the event: Marina Ochos of the Archdiocese Patrimony Office and a member of the Foundation board and Roberto Torres of the State Archives Office.

Vignette 15

Over the 30 years, hundreds of folks—from Santa Fe, throughout New Mexico and beyond—became members of the Guadalupe Historic Foundation. They paid simple annual dues whether as individuals, families and/or businesses, both big and small, to support the Foundation in its on-going efforts to save the Santuario. Their numbers are legion, their devotion still appreciated.

Vignette 16:

Finally, what was accomplished? For one, the Santuario exists today because of the dedicated efforts of hundreds, perhaps thousands, of people... many of whom are listed in the Appendices. On the record, the Foundation was awarded the (Santa Fe) Mayor's award for Excellence in the Arts/Cultural Preservation in 2001.

At that time, the Foundation board named honorary members whose names you've seen elsewhere because they excelled above and beyond the calling to which the others also had responded. The honorary board members selected were Monsignor Leo Lucero, Concha Ortiz y Pino de Kleven, Dr. Gabrielle Palmer, Sir John Herklotz, Jim Meeker, Robert Martin and Edward Gonzales.

Vignette 17

Special dedication goes to Pat Gonzales y Gonzales, who, with her husband, Edward, has persevered over the years to support the Santuario de Guadalupe and its story. They join the hundreds of volunteers who saved the Santuario and made the miracle real for all of Santa Fe.

A Brief History of the Guadalupe Historic Foundation

he Guadalupe Historic Foundation was incorporated as a non-for-profit New Mexico corporation on February 28, 1975. The Foundation was granted tax-exempt status as a 501©3 non-profit by the IRS. Overall direction of the Santuario de Guadalupe is vested in a board of trustees composed of the following interested noted local citizens:

Leo E. Lucero, President. Father Lucero is pastor of Our Lady of Guadalupe Parish in Santa Fe. He has been, and is, active in various civic and religious activities, including the Santa Fe Chamber Music Festival.

Mariano Romero, Vice President. Mr. Romero is director of bilingual education for the Santa Fe Public Schools. He holds degrees from the College of Santa Fe (BA) and the University of New Mexico (MA).

Gabrielle Palmer, Secretary/Treasurer. Dr, Palmer is a graduate of the University of the Americas, Mexico City (BA), and the University of New Mexico (MA, PhD). She is an active historian and author.

Robert F. Sanchez is archbishop of the Santa Fe, New Mexico, Archdiocese. He is a graduate of Immaculate Heart of Mary Seminary, Santa Fe, and Gregorian University at the North American College in Rome, Italy.

Clara Apodaca is the First Lady of New Mexico. She is the wife of Gov. Jerry Apodaca and a graduate of the University of New Mexico.

Saul Cohen is a practicing attorney in Santa Fe, New Mexico. He is a graduate of UCLA (BA) and the Stanford School of Law (JD).

Van Deren Coke is director of the University of New Mexico Art Museum. He is a graduate of the University of Kentucky (BA) and Indiana University (MFA), as well as an art historian and noted author and photographer.

Benjamin Padilla is CEO of the Manuel Lujan Insurance Agency in Santa Fe, New Mexico. He is a graduate of the General of America School for Insurance Agents and active in civic affairs in the City Different.

Foundation staff is composed of a director, associate director and part-time help. They are aided by a host of volunteers.

Gabrielle Palmer, Director. The director is responsible to the Board of Trustees for the overall direction of the Santuario, its general administration and policy, the planning of exhibits and cultural events and fund-raising on a national level.

Nancy Carroll, Associate Director. The associate director is responsible for the physical administration of the Santuario, including part-time staff and volunteers, as well as the logistics of exhibits and cultural events, membership drive and fund-raising efforts at the local level.

William Field, former chief designer for the Polaroid Corporation, handles all design work for the Foundation and Santuario and serves as a consultant on exhibits.

Richard Wilder, a registered landscaper, is in charge of maintenance.

The Guadalupe Historic Foundation
Presidents and Directors

Year	President	Director
1975–1978	Father Leo Lucero	Gabrielle Palmer
1979–1980	Father Leo Lucero	Jose Griego y Maestas
1981	Michael Branch	Virginia Castellano
1982	Peter J. Gomez, Jr.	Virginia Castellano
1983–1984	Gregory Salinas	Virginia Castellano
1985–1987	Marina Ochoa	Virginia Castellano
1988–1989	Edward "Gonzo" Gonzales	Lorraine Goldman
1990–1992	Antonio de Pedro	Emilio "Gabby" Ortiz
1993	Miquela Anaya	Emilio Ortiz
1994	Ray Herrera	Emilio Ortiz
1995–1997	Joe Martinez	Emilio Ortiz
1998	Donald J. Ortiz	Emilio Ortiz
1999–2003	Leo Kahn	Emilio Ortiz

2004–January 31, 2006 Leo Kahn and board, after Emilio Ortiz's death

The Guadalupe Historic Foundation Board of Trustees (1975–2006)

The Guadalupe Historic Foundation Volunteers (1975–2005) Partial List

Cecilia Abeyta	Virginia Clark	Nicole Latham
Joe Aceves	Michelle Cohen	Helen Longacre
Eutilia Alarid	Craig Dell	Steven Lowe
Ike Alarid	Gene Doty	Cesaria Lujan
Aluaria Apodaca	Rosina Escuder	Clara Lujan
Becky Archuleta	Vicenta Espinosa	Lucile McCulloch
Edward Archuleta	Jane Flynn	Bill McGonigle
Matt Armijo	John Flynn	Mae McMenemon
Phillip Baca	George Gallegos	Ernie B. Martinez
Margaret Bailer	Dora Garcia	Raymond Martinez
Janice Blevins	Ed Garcia	Theresa Martinez
Juanita Bloch	Becky Gonzales	Jo McCrossen
Placido Borrego	Elidoro Gonzales	Lena McQuithy
Mary Boshen	Pat G. Gonzales	Linder Meaders
Susan Breckenridge	Dennis Hammond	Barbara Meem
Amelia Brown	Fay Herta	Jeanette Miller
Pauline Brown	Helen Herta	Oswald Montoya
Anna Bryson	Bernadine Hesch	Rafaelita Montoya
Betty Burkhart	Larry Holgerson	Waldy Montoya
Marie Byrne	Patty Johnston	Dolores Quintana Myers
Robin Carlson	Maxie Jones	Rosalie Nava
Teresa Castanon	Grace Kimball	Ray Nichols
Joey Chaurz	Ava Larragoite	Helmut Numeer
Vicki Chaurz	Nancy LaFortune	Albert Ortiz
Jordie Chilson	Dr. Enrique La Madrid	Eduvigen Ortiz

Jerry Ortiz
Louie Ortiz
Marcella Ortiz
Rumalda Ortiz
Marianne O'Shaughnessy
Eva Pacheco
Tommy Padilla
Diane Pearson
Luisa Penner
Loretta Dolores Perez
Angela Pino
Dick Pino
Rose Press
Carmen Quintana
Dede Quintana
Henrietta Quintana
Pete Quintana
Mary Louise Rawls
Estelle Rebec
Sarah Richardson
Valentina Rivera
Carlota Rodriguez
Frank Rodriguez
Eleanor Rohr-Bacher
Teresa Romero

Malinda Saiz
Rose Sandoval
Gabriel Sandoval
Debra Snyderman
Helen Sosaya
Henrietta Stocker
Barbara Sumner
Clare Tallman
Dorothea Tallman
Ruth Thomas
Anthony Trujillo
Mardell Ortiz Trujillo
Roland Trujillo
Tomas Valdez
Anna Vieira
Dorothy Vieira
Frances Vieira
Pat Vigil
Dorothy Wade
Nell Watts
Charlotte White
Joaquina Wilson
Jim Wofford
Ernest Zapata
Barbara Zook

THE GUADALUPE HISTORIC FOUNDATION DONORS (1975–2005) PARTIAL LIST

Donors

Kathleen Abeles
Richard Abeles
Sean Abram
Herman Agoyo
Tomasita Aguilar
Anthony Alarid
Frank Alarid
June Alarid
Theresa Alarid
Jannie Allen
Dewey Anderson
Kenneth Anglemire
Anthony's at the Delta/Espanola
Archbishop Michael J. Sheehan
Jake Archuleta
Victoria Nova Archuleta
Joseph Armbruster
Art Horizons, Ltd./Maurice Loriaux
Art in Eldorado
Art Service of Santa Fe
Burch Ault
Mary Avoy
B&G Automotive
B. Dalton Bookseller
Eddie Baca

Frances Baca
Josephine Baca
Matthew Baca
Phillip Baca
Drew Bacigalupa
Richard Bantz
Ralph Barajas
Rutgers Barclay
Mary Barker
M. S. Barton
Betty Bauer
Beckers Delicatessen
Janie Begs
Ervin Bergman
Signe Bergman
Jean Berinati
E. B. Berkley
John Berkley
Alice Ann Biggerstaff
Mathilde Bird
Bishop's Lodge
Debora Bluestone
Bill Bobb
Sande Bobb
Borrego Construction

Barbara Bowman
Elenn Bradbury
Mary Brennan
Brother Claude Lane
Brother Placid Stuckenshneider
Madge Buckley
Bill Buckholtz
Bernardo C de Baca
Joe Carr
Ken Campbell
Candy Man
Joe Carr
Neil Carter
Thayer Carter
G. L. Castillo/Guadalupe Castillo
Johnny Cata
Century Bank of Santa Fe
Mike Cerletti
Richard D. Cermak
Bob Chavez
Ubaldo Chavez
Coca Cola Co.
College of Santa Fe/alumni
Charles Collier
Daniel Colombe
Community Bank of Santa fe
Mary Lou Cook
Liz Cope
James Cordova
Ed Crocker
Estella Cubero
Das Krishna Dass
Ram Dass
Davis and Assoc./Marc Brenan
Peter Dechert
Dee's Restaurant

Ken Delapp
Linda Delgado
De Pedro International
Doodlet's
Dennis Downey
Jacqueline Dunnington
Galen Duran
Sarah Duran
Eldorado Hotel
Enthios Gallery
Pam Epple
Wspanola Abstract Co., Inc.
Clarissa Pinkola Estes
Estevans Restaurant
Tony Eubanks
Father Estaban Anticoli
Father William Hart McNichols
Father Richard Russo
First Interstate Bank of Santa Fe
Viola Fisher
Janie and Glenn Frey
Betty Frosh
Alyce Frank
Jane Flynn
Frame Crafters
Tillie Gabaldon
Woody Gallaway
R. A. Gallegos
Ronnie Gallegos
Pete Garcia
Gas Company of New Mexico
James George
Robin Gideon
Belarmino (Blackie) Gonzales
Pauline Gomez
Cecilia (Teeter) Gonzales

Jack Goode
Barbara Graves
Peggy Grinnell
Guadalupe Credit Union
Guadalupe Street Merchants
Association
Rosemary Gurule
John Hachmula
Gail Haggard
Monica Sosaya Halford
Jim Hans
Richard Hartshorne
Rabbi Leonard Helman
Bill Herrera
Charlie Herrera
Frank Herrera
Jake Herrera
Joe J. Herrera
Martha and Martina Herrera
Ruben Hesch
Hispanic Cultural Center of Albu-
querque/Edward and Virginia Lujan
Historic Santa Fe Foundation
Annabelle Hoffman
Maya Hoffman
Hotel St. Francis
Howard Johnson
Richard Hubbell
Schatzie Hubbell
Cornelia Hull
Jo Huntington
Inn at Loretto
Inn of The Anasazi
Inn of The Governors
Inn On The Alameda
IRES Society

Jackalope
Myra Ellen Jenkins
Josie's Casa de Comida
KHVM Radio
KMIK Radio
KNME TV
Chris Krahling/ New Mexico Bicen-
tennial Commission
KTRC Radio/Bill Handrahan
KVSF/Bob Barth
La Fonda Hotel
La Posada de Santa Fe Resort & Spa
La Tertulia Restaurant
Land of Enchantment Credit Union
Mike Langer
LANL Foundation of Los Alamos
Thomas Lark
Marian Lane
Las Cosad Kitchen Shop
Nicole Latham
Elle Chavez de Leitner
Ellen de Chavez Litner
Carlos Lopez
Conchita Lopez
Cruz Lopez
Jose Lopez
Owen Lopez
Lopez Roofing
Inn at Loretto Gift Shop
Stephen Lucero
Edward Lujan
Lujan Insurance
Manuel Lujan, Jr.
Stephan Lucero
Marian Love
Lynnell's

M. Maranon

Virginia Mackey

E. A. (Tony) Mares

Mela and Robert Martin

Esther Martinez

Irene Martinez

Father Jerome Y Alire Martinez

Ralph Martinez

Dan McBride

Marian Frank McCandless

Jo McCrossen

McCune Foundation

Bill McGonigle

Tom McGuire

Tim McNeill

Linda Meaders

Joe M. Medina

Saul Medina

Antonio Mendoza

Menetrey Enterprises

Adela Miera

Bill Miller

Montez Familia

Richard (Dickie) Montoya

Ed Moreno

Jeremy Morrelli

Mountain Bill Community Relations
  Team

Mr. Tax

G. E. Mullan

Claire Munzenrider

Kammer Musik

National Catholic Women

New Mexico Community Foundation

Ann Noble

Phil Naumber

Ralph E. Nava

New Mexico State Highway Department

Jim O'Brian

Jim O'Hara

Old Santa Fe Association

Tom Olivas

David Olson

Open Hands of Santa Fe

Ortega Wood Work

Ortiz Printing/Ralph Ortiz

Our Lady of Guadalupe Ladies Society

Our Lady of Guadalupe Parish Council

Marco (Mark) Oviedo

Pat Oviedo

Ana Pacheco

Irene Padilla

Orlando Padilla

Palace Restaurant

Y. A. Paloheimo

Pasqual's Restaurant

Daniel Thomas Paulos

PBA Mail Service

Bob Pepper

Luis Perea, Jr.

Diane Perez

Pflueger's Shoe Store

Dave Phillips

Maggie Phinney

Karl-Heinz Planitz

Plaza Galleria

Phase 1 Realty

Anthony Portago

Danny Porter

Frank Porter

Nicholas Potter

Robyn Powell

Concha Quintana
Henrietta Quintana
Rare Bear of Santa Fe
Recursos de Santa Fe
Charles (Chuck) Reynolds
Dorothy Mary Rhoads
Reynaldo (Sonny) Rivera
Michael Roach
Ida Edith Romero
Leo Romero
Ruben Romero
Phillip Roybal
Richard Roybal
Rudy Fernandez Realty
Carl Bryant Rogers
Paula Rodriguez
Norman Sackett
Richard Salazar/New Mexico State
  Historian
Jonathan Sandoval
Santa Fe Art Board
Santa Fe Council for the Arts, Inc./
  Larry Ogan
Santa Fe Hilton Hotel
Santa Fe Neighborhood Housing
  Services
Curtis F. Schaafsma
Kendall Scott
Jane Sear
Arlene Cisneros Sena
Jojo Sena
Ron Shirley
Chris Sims
Sister Veronica Brutosky
Sister Rita Keshock

Sister Giotto Moots
Sister Mary Grace Thul
Shoetime
Joe Sisneros
David Smith
Hastings Smith
Miguel C. Leatham Smith
David Snow
St. Bernadette Institute of Sacred Art
Arthur Smith
Paul Spangle
State Employees Credit Union
Stanford Art Committee
Myrtle Stedman
John Stephenson
Cynthia Stibolt
STO Industries
Southwest Bank of Santa Fe
Dolores Sullivan
Brown Sutin
Thayer Sutin
Taco Bell of Santa Fe
Jeff Tafnors
Jerry Tapia
Luis Tapia
Michael Taylor
Ten Thousand Waves
The Albuquerque Journal North
Bradley A. Tepaske
The Friends of The Desert Chorale
The Sheraton Inn
The Shop/Christmas/Ed Berry
The Santa Fe Reporter
The Santa Fean Magazine
Miguel Lea Tham

Anita Gonzales Thomas
Tibetan Monks from Gyudmed of
  Southern India
Kubda Tigges
Joseph V. Toschi
Tony Truesdale
Melvin Trujillo
Michael Trujillo
Pete Trujillo
Frank Turley
Turner Carroll Gallery
Sabino Ulibarri
University of New Mexico/Stanley
  Rhine
Michael Urioste
U. S. West/Community Relations
Eli Valdez
Valdes Paint & Glass
Varella Realty
Peter Vaughn
Pablita Velarde
Glen Velez
Federico Vigil
Leonard Vigil
Kathy Wagner
Weavers' Guild
Wellborn Paint Store
Katherine Wells
Eric Werner
White Swan Linen
Wilson Transfer & Storage
Wind River Trading Co.
Daniel Wolfe
Hans Wright
David Berthier Yarbrough

Ginny York
Mardes York
Susan & Daniel Young
Michael (Mike) Zolpe

Major Donors

Alpine Builders Supply
Archdiocese of Santa Fe/Archbishop
  Robert F. Sanchez
Maria Benitez
U. S. Bicentennial Commission
Bishop Lamy Fund
Bradbury & Stamm Contractors
Carpenters Union 1353
Carrier Air Conditioning of Santa Fe/
  Cliff Crouch
Casa Allegre Garden club
City of Santa Fe/Philip Baca
City of Santa Fe Arts Commission
City of Santa Fe Mayor's Award
Father Crispin Butz
Louis Frosh
Gene Gallegos
Dolores & Leo R. Gomez
Stanford Goodkin
John Herklotz
Concha Ortiz y Pino de Kleven
KSWV Radio of Santa Fe
Ray Latham
Los Artesanos Imports Co.
Jean & Manuel Lujan
Manuel Lujan, Sr.
Willie Lynch
Marielle & Robert McKinney
Jim Meeker
Monsimer Foundation
Mountain Bell/George Gillespie
Nathaniel Owings
Kenny Passarelli
PCI Contractors, Inc./Gilbert &

Pauline Duran
Puertas de Santa Fe
Rancho Encantado/Betty and John
Egan
Joe Schepps
Abe Silver
Jacqueline Smith
Stan Davis & Associates
State of New Mexico/Grant and
Heritage Preservation Award
Jean & Joseph Sullivan
Goodwin Taylor
The Santa Fe New Mexican
The University of New Mexico/
Maxwell Museum of Anthropology
U. S. National Endowment for the Arts
Valdes Corp.
Walmart of Santa Fe

Presentations and Exhibits at the Santuario

Musical/Drama Presentations

Margaret (Peggy) Abbott
Antonia Apodaca
Nancy Arnon
ARS Nova Chamber Singers
Janelle Ayon
Baile Folklorico de Denver, CO
Ballet Folklorico de Santa Fe
Marilyn Barnes
Boyd Barrett
Steve Bell
Susan Blinderman
Robin H. Bowen/KHVM Radio
Maria Benitez Teatro Flamenco
Caballeros de Vargas Santa Fe
Luis Campos
Lili Castillo
Tibo Chavez, Jr.
Chesapeake Trio
Sounds True/Sarah Chestnutt
Chorus Singers of Los Alamos
Chorus Singers of Phoenix (Metro)
Coro de Camara
Harry Cowel
Danzas Espanelas/Maestro Antonio
  Triana

Elizabeth Lynne Dickey
Charly Drobeck
El Rancho de Las Golondrinas
Fayette Street Academy
Peter Garland
Phillip Gloss
Grimmel College
Ron Grinaie
Nancy L. Harper
Ronald Hays
Houston (TX) Children's Chorus
Karen Hutchinson
Joseph Illick
Kate Jewel
Tara Jimenez y Morales
Anna Kaltenbach
Kammer Musik
Peter Kater
Norman Krieger
Amy LaLime
Nancy Lauphemier
Los Ninos Cantores de Santa Fe/
  Antonio Avila
Virginia Mackey
De Warrt Marco

E. A. (Tony) Mares
Antonio Mendoza
Mikaeli Chamber Choir of Stockholm. Sweden
Van Ann Moore
Musica de Camara of Santa Fe
New Mexico Folklore Society
Andre Garcia Nuthmann
Kenny Passarelli
Linda Piper
Pro Coro
Pytel-Zak
Lin Raymond
Terry Riley
Ruben Romero
Sangre de Christo Chorale/Molly Ferber
Santa Fe Chamber Ensemble
Santa Fe Desert Chorale/Larry Bandsfield
Santa Fe Fiesta Council
Santa Fe Music Conservatory
Santa Fe Stages
Santa Fe Women's Ensemble
Santa Fe Symphony
Eric Satie
Robb Scott
Steven Scott
Robert Segovia
Serenata of Santa Fe/Maestro James Raphael
Sipapu Foundation
Southwest Chamber Trio
Steel Point Threatre
Taos Chamber Music

The Ensemble of Santa fe/Tomas O'Connor
The Gay Men's Chorus of Albuquerque
The Holy Trinity Chorale Group
The Vaughn Trio
Ann Waldman
Waldorf School
William Weldon
Kevin Zoering

ART EXHIBITS AT THE SANTUARIO

Frank Alarid
Jake Archuleta
Bernardo C de Baca
Charlie Carrillo
James Cordova
Linda Daboub
Christine DeCamp
Montez Familia
R A Gallegos
John Huckmala
Mark Kane
Ellen Chavez de Litner
Los Artisanos
Ted Lukits
John Meig
Irene Nicolas
Northern New Mexico Weavers
Ortega Woodwork
Dan Paulos
Louise Roach
St. Bernadette Institute
Eric Werner
Sandra Duran Wilson

Acknowledgments

*N*o writer, whether of fiction or non-fiction, works alone. Others provide inspiration, instruction and information. This recognizes those who directly guided me in bringing this book to fruition.

First and foremost is Edward Gonzales. Indeed, I would not have known of the remarkable history of the Guadalupe Historic Foundation were it not for this Norteno. Edward introduced me to others with whom he worked at the Foundation over 20 years and they, in turn, shared their time and information. They include:

Gail Delgado, current director of the Santuario, told me "if it weren't for the Foundation, we wouldn't be here today."

Gilbert Duran, contractor and owner of PCI Contractors, Inc., completed exterior restoration, including the roof, of the Santuario more than 25 years ago.

Felice Gonzales, lawyer and Foundation board of trustees legal representative, guided the board through various legal mazes over the years.

Ray Herrera brought together family members, Alpine Lumber, the Carpenters Union and Foundation members years ago to install the existing flooring in the Santuario. "I belong to the Cathedral (home parish, Cathedral Basilica of St. Francis of Assisi), but my heart is here (the Santuario)," Herrera said.

Leo Kahn, an accountant and retired chief financial officer of the New Mexico Department of Health, successfully guided the Foundation to its closure on Jan. 31, 2006, as its last president and director.

Gabrielle Palmer, noted Spanish Colonial and art historian, initiated the fund-raising effort to save the Santuario and became one of the two founders and first director of the Foundation.

Catherine (Cathie) Zacher—teacher, entrepreneur and leader of several non-profit organizations and first woman member of the Santa Fe Rotary—used her many skills on behalf of the Foundation as a board member.

Sometimes, people are helpful without realizing how much help they have been. These include Anne Hillerman who, like me, is a journalist and now is writing suspenseful, successful fiction; Ana Pacheco, a City of Santa Fe historian and writer; and Roslyn Pulitzer, copy editor and photographer whose eye catches everything and misses nothing.

Then, there is Jim Smith, editor, publisher and friend extraordinaire.

Finally, thank you all, seen and unseen, who helped make this book possible, including an earlier writer who asked of Our Lady: Guide my heart, my mind and my hand.

CPSIA information can be obtained
at www.ICGtesting.com
Printed in the USA
FSOW01n2229261216
28800FS